BEANSTALK'S BASICS FOR PIANO

TECHNIQUE BOOK
PREPARATORY
LEVEL B

FINGER GYM
2:38
HOME 27   VISITOR 26

BY CHERYL FINN AND EAMONN MORRIS

WILLIS MUSIC

12462

FINGER GYM EVENTS

Warm-Up! 3
Running Relay 4
Doing Somersaults 5
Swaying Back & Forth 6
Spinning Around 7
Tire Walk! 8
Daddy Long-Leg Steps 9
Sack Relay 10
Hopping on the Spot! 11
Jumping Rope 12
Rolling 13
Floor Hockey Warm-Ups! 14
Running Up & Down 15
Stiff-Finger March! 16
Finger Hopping 17
Spins! 18
Stepping Back & Forth 19
Simon Says… 20
Cross Country Run 21
Piggyback Ride 22
Walking & Hopping 23
Playing Hopscotch 24
Two-Fingered Hop! 25
Running Through Tires 26
Flat Tire Relay 27
Playing Basketball 28
Stretching 29
Short Sprints 30
Drag Race 31
Obstacle Course! 32

PARENTS, STUDENTS AND TEACHERS! WELCOME TO THE FINGER GYM!

The performance of daily technical exercises is an essential part of piano training. Like an athlete, the pianist cannot perform to full capability without proper physical conditioning.

Beanstalk's Basics for Piano Technique takes the student's fingers into the gym every day for a series of exercises and games taken right out of gym class! These **Finger Gym** workouts not only improve finger dexterity, independence, control, stamina, hand position, style and musicianship, but also help to stimulate musical imagination.

Beanstalk's Basics for Piano Technique uses colorful stickers to reward a job well done. As with the lesson book we recommend that the teacher remove the sticker sheet as the student begins each book. This preserves the element of surprise and increases motivation.

Consideration of the ***Music Maker*** reward stickers for each exercise is ideally withheld until the student has first mastered the basic elements of the music in question such as key signature, time signature, notes and rhythm.

Each **Finger Gym** page corresponds directly with the material covered in ***Beanstalk's Basics for Piano Lesson Books*** and works to further reinforce the technical challenges introduced.

Finger Gym contains another motivational tool known as ***'Coach's Corner'***. Here the student is challenged to perform and record several repetitions of each exercise. We encourage students to perform their 'repetitions' five days each week with the remaining two days left to parents' and teachers' discretion.

We wish much success and enjoyment to all **Finger Gym** participants!

To
Alanna & Brianne

CHERYL FINN

EAMONN MORRIS

12462

This piece contains intervals of a 2nd.

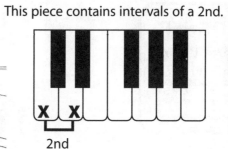

2nd

MUSIC MAKER

1. Gentle arm swings.

Smoothly

WARM - UP!

$f-p$

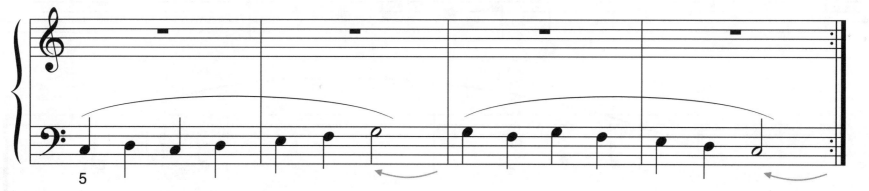

5

ARM SWINGS

To add finesse and musicality to your playing, try adding **ARM SWINGS**. In this series, arm swings are marked with arrows ( ) showing the direction of the swing (Swing arm out **RIGHT** : Swing arm out **LEFT** :). **SLOWLY** and **GENTLY** move your arm out, away from your sides for the value of the given note. Then **GRACEFULLY** lift off the key. It's like drawing a happy face with your elbow!

RUNNING RELAY

CORRESPONDS WITH PAGES 4 AND 5 OF BEANSTALK'S LESSON BOOK PREP B.

4

12462

This piece contains intervals of a 3rd.

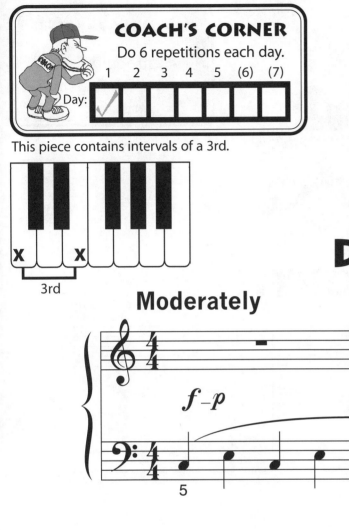

3rd

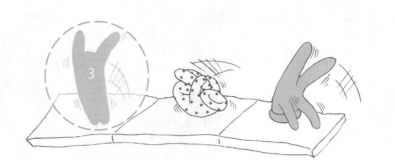

DOING SOMERSAULTS

Moderately

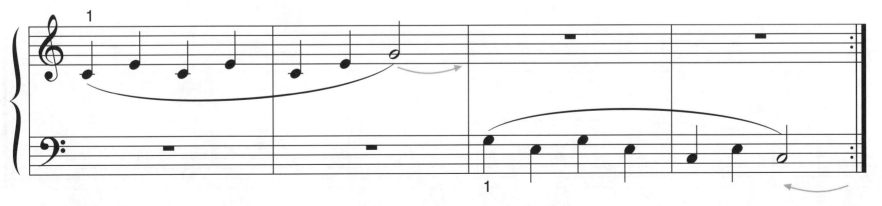

TECH TIP REMINDER

Hand position is very important when you play. In a good hand position your thumb and 5th finger should **STAND UP** and be strong. (They should not lie flat or curl up!)

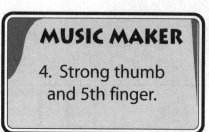

MUSIC MAKER

4. Strong thumb and 5th finger.

Moderately

SWAYING BACK & FORTH

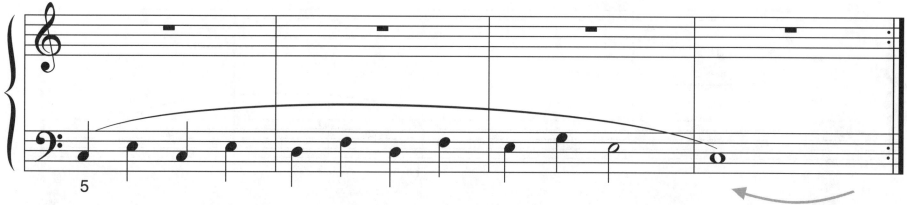

CORRESPONDS WITH PAGES 7 AND 8 OF BEANSTALK'S LESSON BOOK PREP B.

TECH TIP REMINDER

An **EVEN TONE** ensures that your playing is **SMOOTH** and shows that you are in control. To develop an even tone, play each note in the passage with the same loudness ~ no bumps or weak notes! Remember to **STAND STRONG** on your thumb and 5th finger tip. Most importantly, **LISTEN** to the sounds that you are creating!

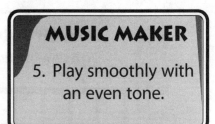

MUSIC MAKER

5. Play smoothly with an even tone.

This piece contains intervals of a 4th.

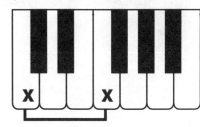

4th

Smoothly

SPINNING AROUND

CORRESPONDS WITH PAGE 9 OF BEANSTALK'S LESSON BOOK PREP B.

IMAGINE you are walking carefully without tripping or stumbling!

TIRE WALK!

Steadily

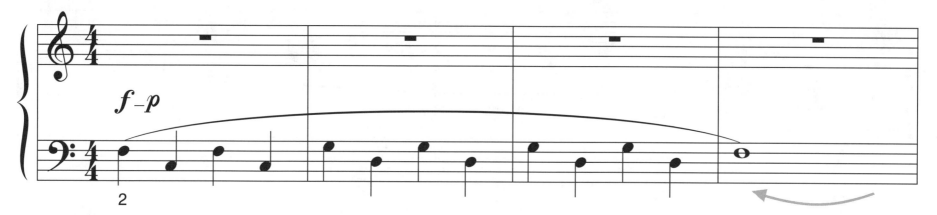

CORRESPONDS WITH PAGES 10 AND 11 OF BEANSTALK'S LESSON BOOK PREP B.

12462

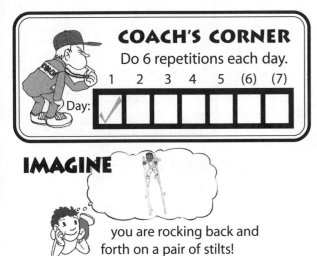

IMAGINE

you are rocking back and forth on a pair of stilts!

This piece contains intervals of a 5th.

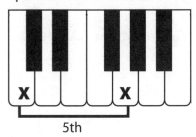

5th

Steadily

DADDY LONG-LEG STEPS

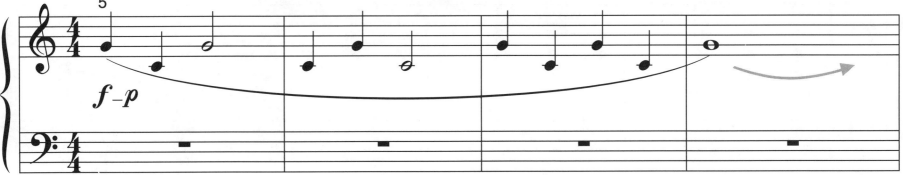

CORRESPONDS WITH PAGE 12 OF BEANSTALK'S LESSON BOOK PREP B.

TECH TIP
When playing an **HARMONIC INTERVAL** you must play both notes **EXACTLY TOGETHER.**

IMAGINE
that you are jumping up and down with your feet tied together!

This piece contains **HARMONIC** intervals of a 2nd, 3rd and 5th.

SACK RELAY

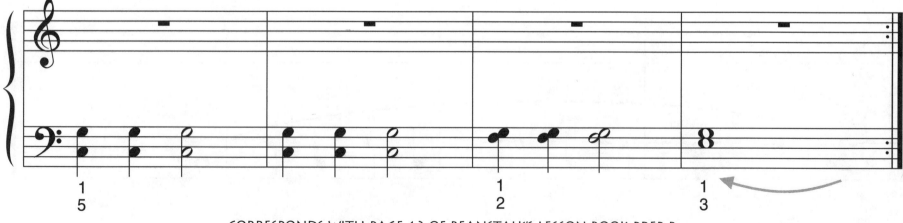

TECH TIP
To make staccatos sound crisp,
BOUNCE from your wrist!

MUSIC MAKER
9. Crisp staccatos.

IMAGINE
that the keys are very
hot!

HOPPING ON THE SPOT!

Crisply

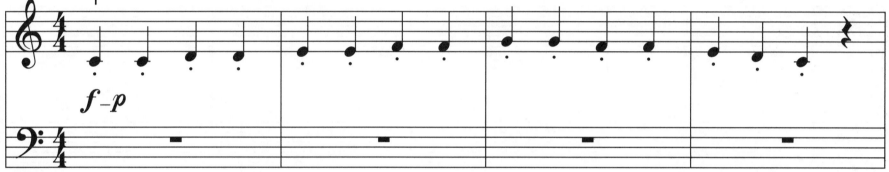

CORRESPONDS WITH PAGE 14 OF BEANSTALK'S LESSON BOOK PREP B.

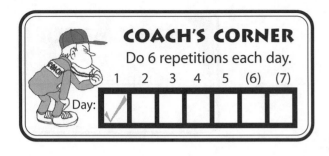
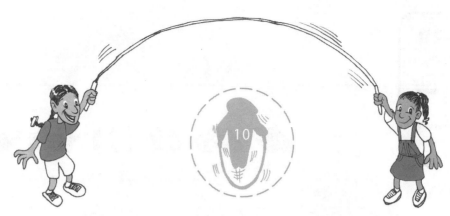

MUSIC MAKER

10. Play exactly together with crisp staccatos.

JUMPING ROPE

Crisply

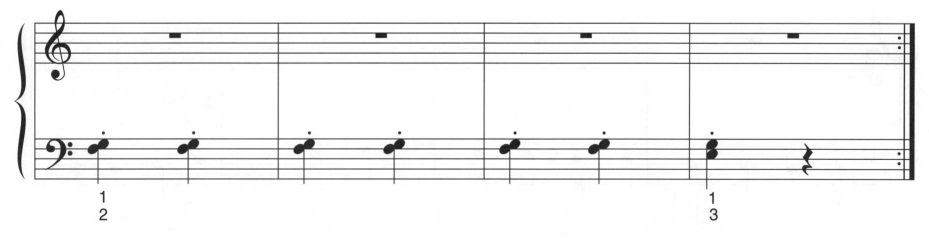

CORRESPONDS WITH PAGES 15 AND 16 OF BEANSTALK'S LESSON BOOK PREP B.

12462

ROLLING

Smoothly

f–p

DOUBLE ARM SWINGS WARM-UP!!!
For this movement, **BOTH** arms swing out gently from your sides at the same time. Here are some **ARM SWING** warm-ups for you to try using both hands.

Count: 1 - 2 - 3 - 4

Count: 1 - 2 - 3

Count: 1 - 2

CORRESPONDS WITH PAGE 17 OF BEANSTALK'S LESSON BOOK PREP B.

MIDDLE C POSITION

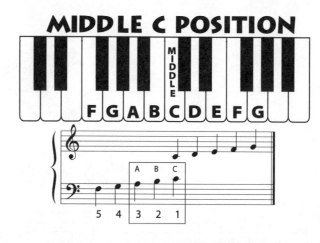

F G A B C D E F G

5 4 3 2 1

MUSIC MAKER

12. Play smoothly with an even tone.

IMAGINE

that each finger has the same strength. Each tone must sound equal all the way up and down.

FLOOR HOCKEY WARM-UPS!

Smoothly

Continue repeating this exercise starting on each C all the way up to the top.

f–p

Smoothly

Continue repeating this exercise starting on each C all the way down to the bottom.

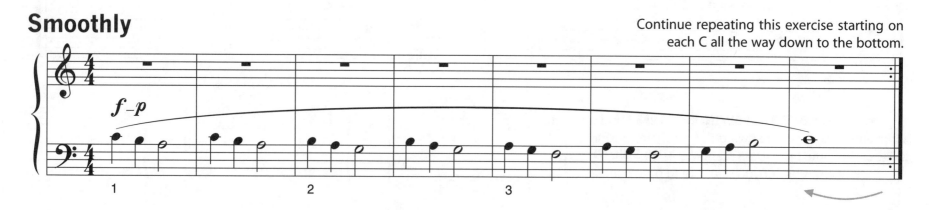

f–p

CORRESPONDS WITH PAGE 18 OF BEANSTALK'S LESSON BOOK PREP B.

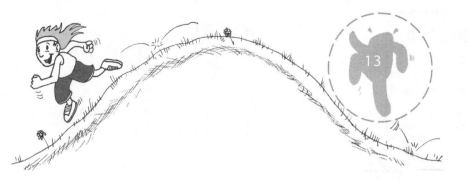

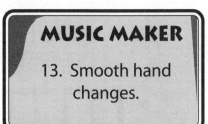

RUNNING UP & DOWN

Smoothly

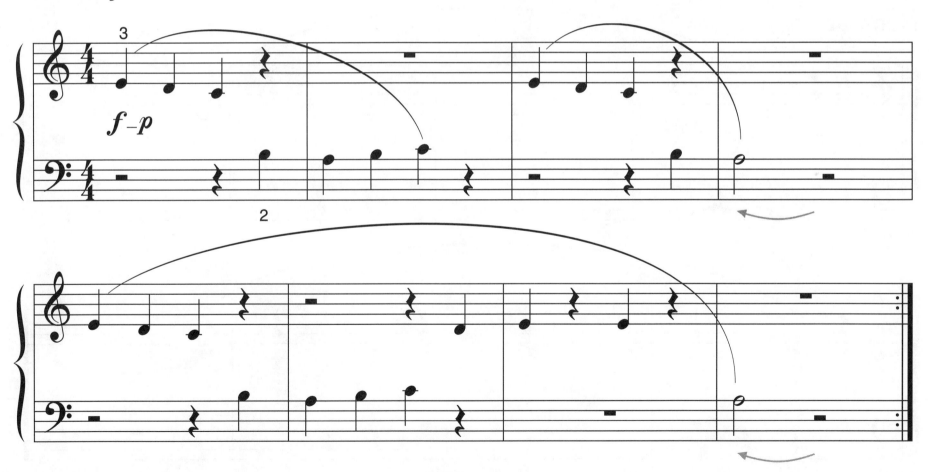

CORRESPONDS WITH PAGE 20 OF BEANSTALK'S LESSON BOOK PREP B.

MUSIC MAKER

15. Crisp staccatos.

Crisply

FINGER HOPPING

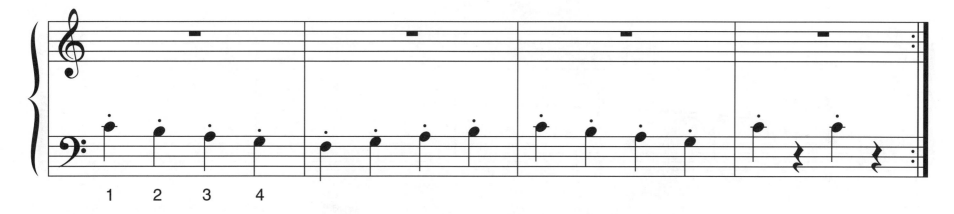

CORRESPONDS WITH PAGE 21 OF BEANSTALK'S LESSON BOOK PREP B.

SPINS!

Smoothly

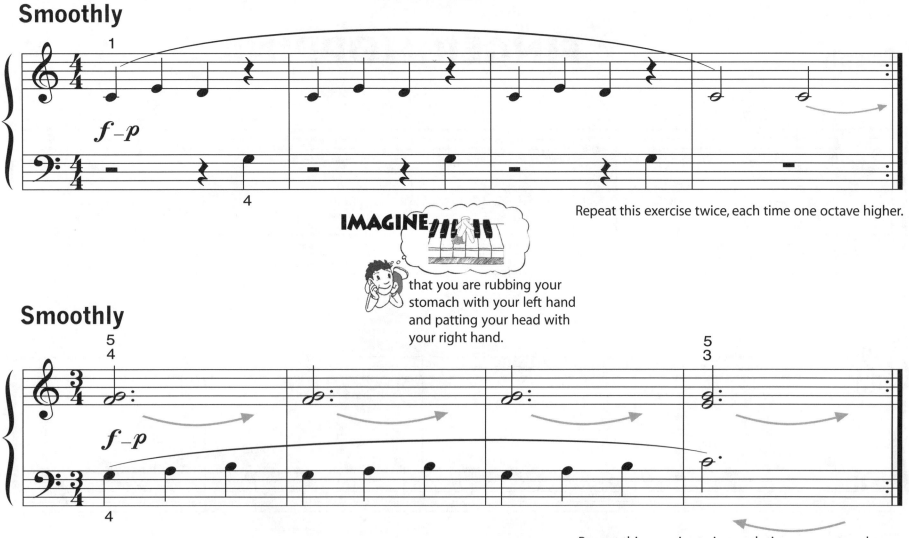

Repeat this exercise twice, each time one octave higher.

IMAGINE that you are rubbing your stomach with your left hand and patting your head with your right hand.

Smoothly

Repeat this exercise twice, each time one octave lower.

CORRESPONDS WITH PAGES 22 AND 23 OF BEANSTALK'S LESSON BOOK PREP B.

MUSIC MAKER

17. Smooth hand changes.

STEPPING BACK & FORTH

Moderately

f – p

1

4

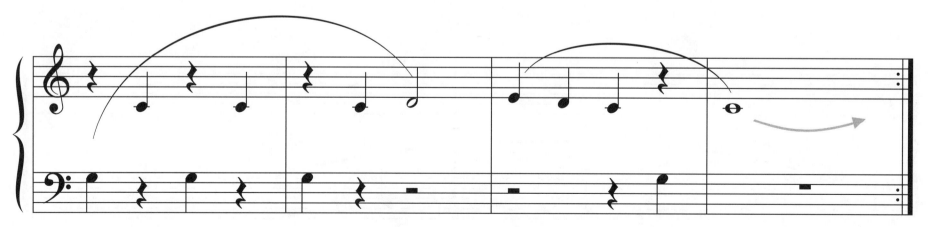

CORRESPONDS WITH PAGE 24 OF BEANSTALK'S LESSON BOOK PREP B.

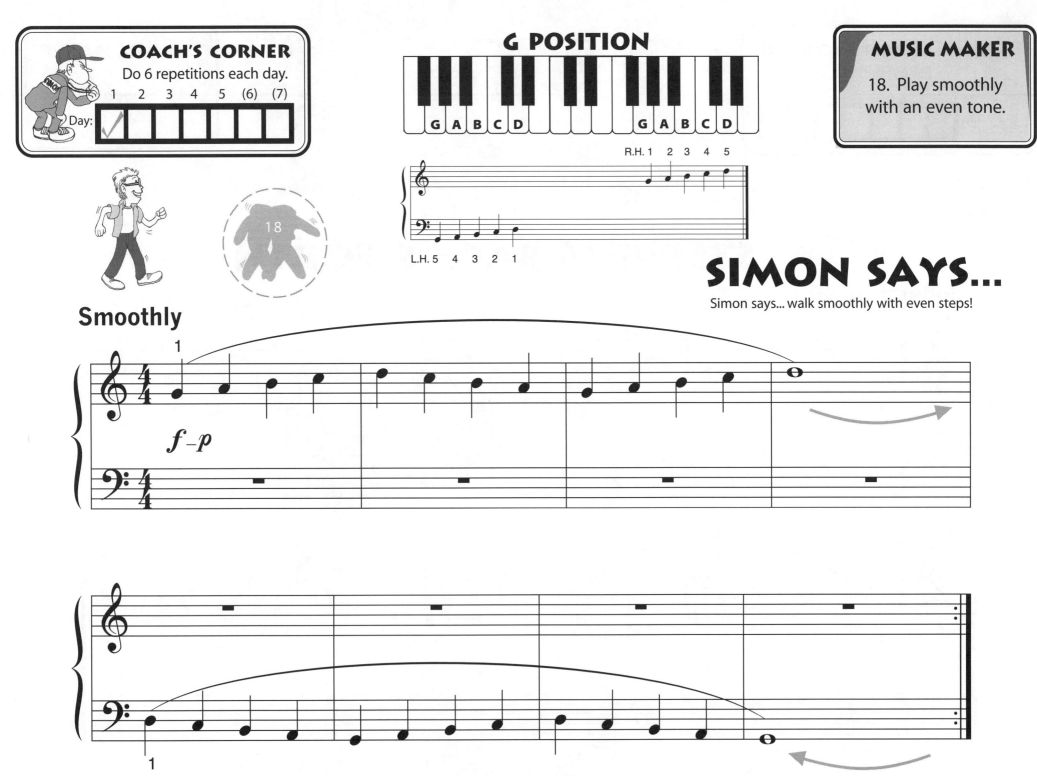

CORRESPONDS WITH PAGE 25 OF BEANSTALK'S LESSON BOOK PREP B.

CROSS COUNTRY RUN

Steadily

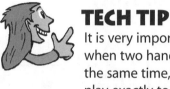

TECH TIP

It is very important that when two hands play at the same time, they play exactly together.

IMAGINE

that you and your best friend are running exactly together!

CORRESPONDS WITH PAGES 26 AND 27 OF BEANSTALK'S LESSON BOOK PREP B.

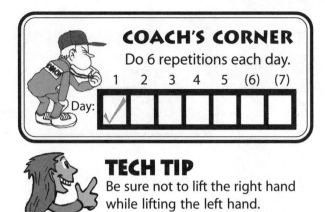

TECH TIP
Be sure not to lift the right hand while lifting the left hand.

MUSIC MAKER
20. Right hand plays smoothly.

IMAGINE

that you are rubbing your stomach with your right hand and patting your head with your left hand!

PIGGYBACK RIDE

Smoothly

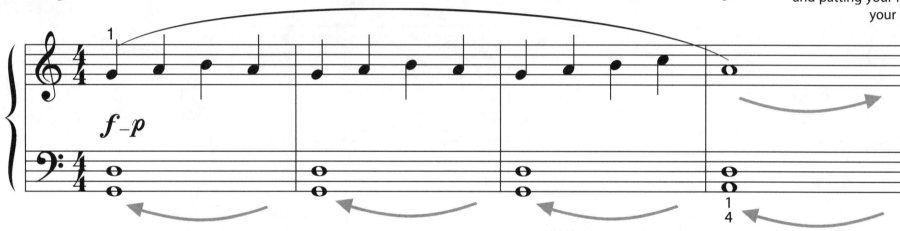

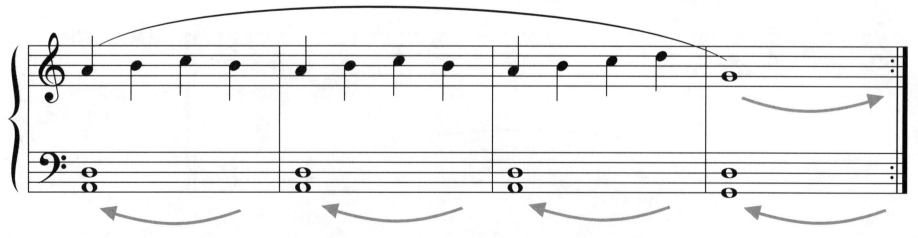

CORRESPONDS WITH PAGE 28 OF BEANSTALK'S LESSON BOOK PREP B.

IMAGINE
walking along and then hopping 3 times!

WALKING & HOPPING

Steadily

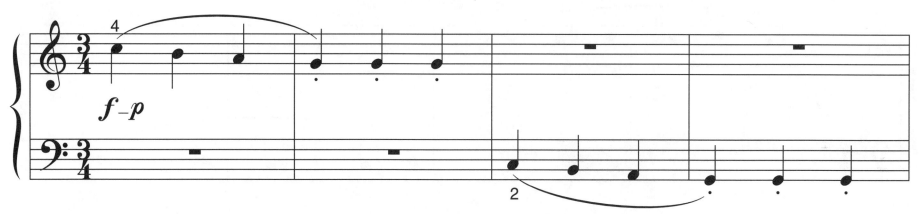

MUSIC MAKER

22. Play legato and staccato.

PLAYING HOPSCOTCH

Steadily

CORRESPONDS WITH PAGE 30 OF BEANSTALK'S LESSON BOOK PREP B.

TWO-FINGERED HOP!

CORRESPONDS WITH PAGE 31 OF BEANSTALK'S LESSON BOOK PREP B.

RUNNING THROUGH TIRES

Smoothly

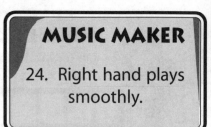

CORRESPONDS WITH PAGES 32 THROUGH 34 OF BEANSTALK'S LESSON BOOK PREP B.

12462

C POSITION

FLAT TIRE RELAY

Moderately

G POSITION

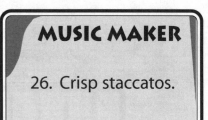

Crisply

PLAYING BASKETBALL

CORRESPONDS WITH PAGE 36 OF BEANSTALK'S LESSON BOOK PREP B.

TECH TIP

Dynamic contrast means moving smoothly from loud to soft or soft to loud. These contrasts make the music more interesting and expressive. For practice try exaggerating your range from very soft to very loud.

MUSIC MAKER

27. Contrast between crescendo and decrescendo.

IMAGINE

starting out at a whisper and working up to a shout.

STRETCHING

Smoothly

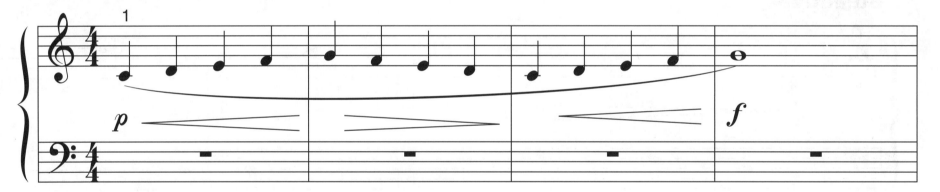

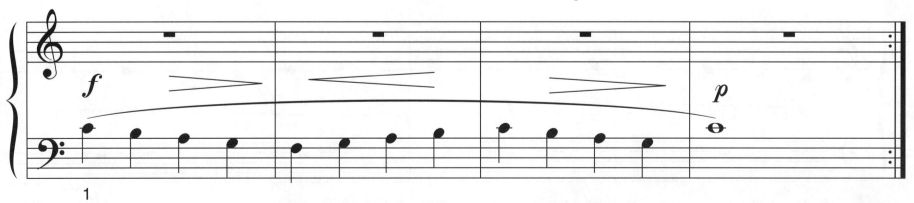

CORRESPONDS WITH PAGE 37 OF BEANSTALK'S LESSON BOOK PREP B.

MUSIC MAKER

28. Contrast between crescendo and decrescendo.

SHORT SPRINTS

Steadily

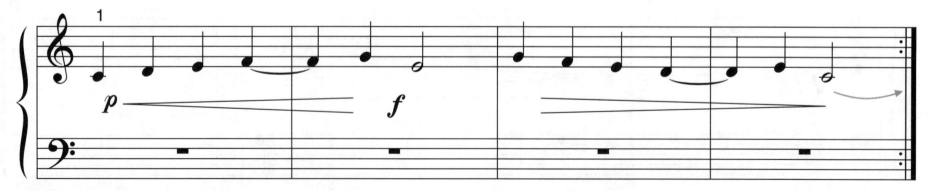

CORRESPONDS WITH PAGES 38 THROUGH 40 OF BEANSTALK'S LESSON BOOK PREP B.

SPORTS DAY!!!

RRAAH! RRAAH! You've made it! Now you're nearly done! Try real hard! We'll cheer you on! Let's have more sports day fun!

MUSIC MAKER

29. Play exactly together with even tones. Play crisp staccatos.

FIRST EVENT

For this first event, imagine that you are dragging one foot and stepping forward with the other!

DRAG RACE

TECH TIP

When connecting harmonic intervals where the bottom note of each interval repeats, join the top note of each interval while lifting the lower note.

Moderately

BLUE RIBBON WINNER!!!

29

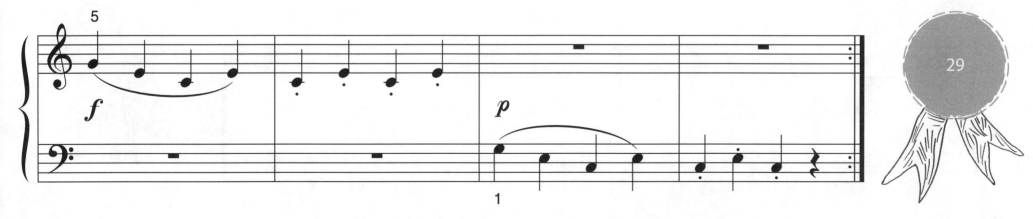

CORRESPONDS WITH PAGES 41 THROUGH 43 OF BEANSTALK'S LESSON BOOK PREP B.

12462

31

SECOND EVENT

For this second event, imagine that you are running an obstacle course! There are tires to run through, ropes to swing from and water to jump across. Be careful not to trip!

MUSIC MAKER

30. Play smoothly with dynamic contrasts. Play crisp staccatos.

OBSTACLE COURSE!

Steadily

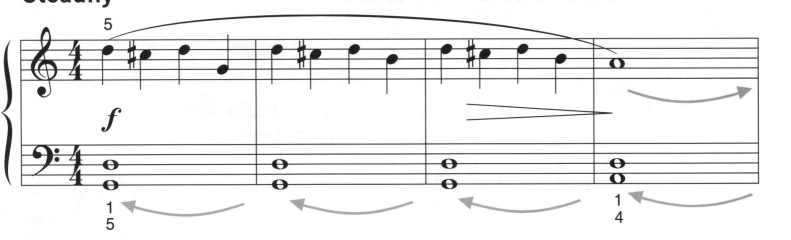

BLUE RIBBON WINNER!!!

CORRESPONDS WITH PAGES 44 AND 45 OF BEANSTALK'S LESSON BOOK PREP B.